THE LEGACY OF
JOHN CYCLONE

Story by Andy J. Weiner

Illustrations by Rick Whipple

RAINTREE
STECK-VAUGHN
RSVP PUBLISHERS

A Harcourt Company

Austin • New York
www.steck-vaughn.com

Library of Congress Cataloging-in-Publication Data
Weiner, Andy, 1988–
    The legacy of John Cyclone / written by Andy Weiner; illustrated
by Rick Whipple.
        p. cm. -- (Publish-a-book)
    Summary: Recalls the amazing feats of John Cyclone, who teethed
on Massachusetts, created the Rocky Mountains when he bumped
his head, and rescued some miners from a huge bear named Fury.
    ISBN 0-7398-2370-1
    1. Children's writings, American. [1. Tall tales. 2. Children's
writings.] I. Whipple, Rick, ill. II. Title. III. Series.

PZ7.W436358 Le 2000
[Fic]--dc21
                                                99-056242

Printed and bound in the United States
1 2 3 4 5   IP   03 02 01 00

This book is dedicated to Ms. Primrose, a great teacher and a reliable friend, and to Ms. Gutman, whose excellent teaching and unique effort helped make this book possible. And, last but not least, this book is dedicated to my special friends, Chris Rizzi and Sam Seifman.— **A.J.W.**

For Sara and Audrey.— **R.W.**

4

Some say John Cyclone was born a natural man, as natural as California's shiniest, most sought-after gold. Others say he was born the most unusual man the universe ever came across.

Take it from me. I know the truth about him. I say he was born ninety percent natural, and ten percent unnatural. Everyone knows he was partly unnatural because when he was one and a half, he teethed on Massachusetts and created Cape Cod. To be able to do this, you can imagine John was pretty big. In fact, John was so large that when he was a baby, he wore a diaper the size of a tablecloth.

Anyway, as John grew, he developed speed, and boy, do
I mean speed. When he was ten, he could make a cheetah
going at seventy miles per hour look like a wagon in a ditch.
And that's how he came to be called John Cyclone.

John was born in Montpelier, Vermont. One day, when he was getting his daily exercise by walking to Denver, Colorado, he broke a hole in the ground just outside of Denver. Lucky for John, he fell into an underground cavern. John walked around. It just so happened that he was right underneath Denver when he banged his head on the roof of the cavern. John had a very strong skull. When John banged his head, Denver shot up one whole mile. You can imagine that many, many, many rocks flew from Denver's rise. If you think this, you're right. The rocks that flew created the Rocky Mountains. John climbed out of the cavern and walked home with an "I'm glad that's over" feeling and a very bad headache.

On his way home, John tripped on the Catskill Mountains in New York. When he fell to the ground, he used one of his hands to catch himself. John lifted his hand as he started crying. His tears, which were very, very, very large, filled up the imprint his fingers made. That is how New York's Finger Lakes came to be.

When John was fifteen, there was a very bad dry spell. But it didn't last too long … thanks to John. He stood up as tall as he could, took some clouds, and squeezed them together to create rain for the crops and plants.

Two years later, there was a famine. Thundering Fury, a giant bear, stole all the food from the fields and nobody could stop him. But the famine lasted only a short time. John's own hard work gave him a great crop that he shared with others, and the famine was history.

Three years later, when John was twenty, the gold rush was in full gear. The only problem was, miners kept disappearing mysteriously. When the news got back East, all the families were thinking the same thing: "Get John to help." One day, a few families came to John to ask for help.

"But I'm only twenty, what can I do?" responded John when he heard their idea.

"John, you're missing the point. You're a 136-foot-high hero. What do you mean, 'What can I do?' You can do something!" pointed out one of the neighbors.

John thought about the idea and said, "You win. I'll do it."

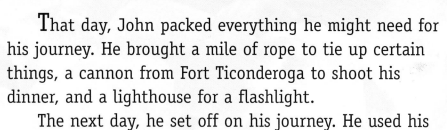

That day, John packed everything he might need for his journey. He brought a mile of rope to tie up certain things, a cannon from Fort Ticonderoga to shoot his dinner, and a lighthouse for a flashlight.

The next day, he set off on his journey. He used his renowned speed and got to California half an hour after he took off from his home. When he arrived, he started looking around. He spotted a note that he picked up and read. It said, "Help! We've been kidnapped and taken to Death Valley." So that's where John went.

When he got there, he fell into a hole. John banged his head again. Only this time the area didn't rise. Instead, there was a loud crack. John got out of the hole and swept away the sand. There was a cave with a boulder blocking the entrance. John moved it like a pebble. Inside were all the miners.

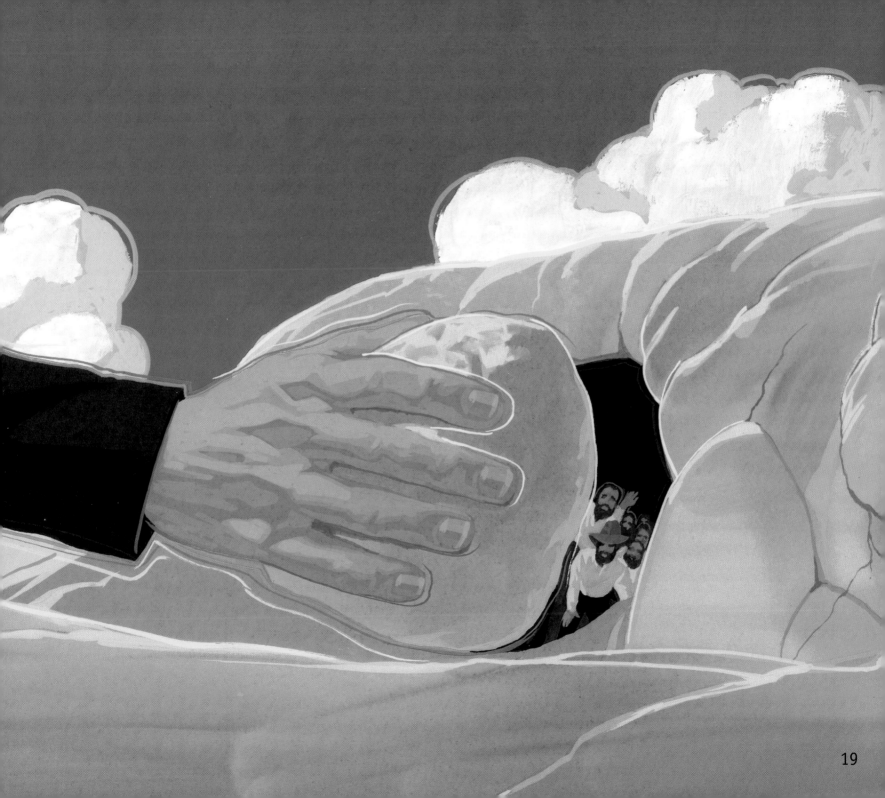

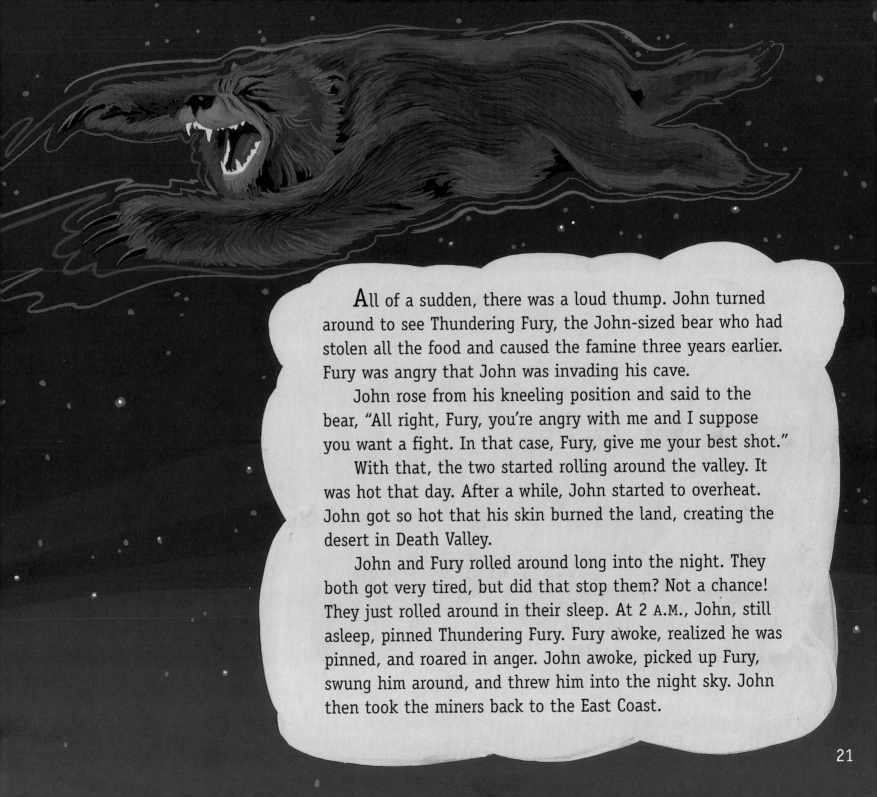

All of a sudden, there was a loud thump. John turned around to see Thundering Fury, the John-sized bear who had stolen all the food and caused the famine three years earlier. Fury was angry that John was invading his cave.

John rose from his kneeling position and said to the bear, "All right, Fury, you're angry with me and I suppose you want a fight. In that case, Fury, give me your best shot."

With that, the two started rolling around the valley. It was hot that day. After a while, John started to overheat. John got so hot that his skin burned the land, creating the desert in Death Valley.

John and Fury rolled around long into the night. They both got very tired, but did that stop them? Not a chance! They just rolled around in their sleep. At 2 A.M., John, still asleep, pinned Thundering Fury. Fury awoke, realized he was pinned, and roared in anger. John awoke, picked up Fury, swung him around, and threw him into the night sky. John then took the miners back to the East Coast.

People say Thundering Fury was never seen again. Not true. When John threw Fury into the sky, the constellation Ursa Major (the Big Dipper) was born. That same constellation can still be seen in the sky on a clear night. Some call it the Big Bear.

Born on November 17, 1988, in Washington, D.C., Andy J. Weiner, author of **The Legacy of John Cyclone**, now lives in Bethesda, Maryland, with his parents, Renee Wohlenhaus and Roger Weiner, who are lawyers at the U.S. Department of Justice. Andy was in the fourth grade at National Presbyterian School in Washington when his writing teacher, Reading Specialist Ms. Anne Gutman, submitted his story about John Cyclone to the Raintree/Steck-Vaughn Publish-a-Book® Contest. At school, Andy likes the creative writing classes taught by Ms. Laura Primrose in the NPS extended day program, and the kickball games with Ms. Jane Kennedy and the kids in "extended day."

Andy enjoys trips to visit his grandparents, Lenora and J.L. Wohlenhaus in Atlantic, Iowa, and Milton and Miriam Weiner, in Lauderhill, Florida. On trips to Rehoboth Beach, Delaware, Andy likes to spend time on the beach, body surfing, and collecting at local shops. Over the past several years, Andy has collected books, trading cards, Beanie Babies, key chains, and Legos. Andy hopes to travel to California, England, and other distant places, especially to visit amusement parks. Free time at home is spent playing video games, building futuristic Lego designs, shooting pool, and, of course, reading. Some of Andy's favorite authors are Jerry Spinelli, Johanna Hurwitz, Franklin W. Dixon, and John Bellairs.

It is hard to predict what Andy will do when he gets older, but he likes school and looks forward to more exciting experiences with his friends at NPS.

The twenty honorable-mention winners in the **1999 Raintree/Steck-Vaughn Publish-a-Book® Contest** were Gabriel Lund, Ball Elementary School, Chatham, IL; Marika Emily Kent, Brookvale Elementary School, Fremont, CA; Brian Velasquez, Mar Vista Elementary School, Aptos, CA; Aaron Vale, Hillel Academy of Broome County, Vestal, NY; Nora Purcell, Barstow Memorial School, Chittenden, VT; Nathan Strauss, Forsyth School, St. Louis, MO; Katie Jasa, Randolph Elementary School, Lincoln, NE; Leslie Laffin, St. Johns Lutheran School, Glendale, WI; Michelle Chapolelaine, Turkey Hill Middle School, Lunenburg, MA; Edward Kurczab, St. James Academy, Totowa, NJ; Kristin Elizabeth Hoffmann, Handley Library, Winchester, VA; Matt Kelly, St. Andrew School, Orlando, FL; Tommy Kusturin, Patten Free Library, Woolwich, ME; Rosemary Cochrane, Queen of Peace School, Ardsley, PA; Ashleigh Hamrick, Ball Elementary School, Chatham, IL; Bronson Arcuri, Melridge Elementary School, Painesville, OH; Samantha Newmark, Mechanicstown School, Middletown, NY; Kate Balic, St. Andrew School, Orlando, FL; Meghan Johnson, Nathan Hale School, Enfield, CT; Samir Kadric, PS 280, Bronx, NY.

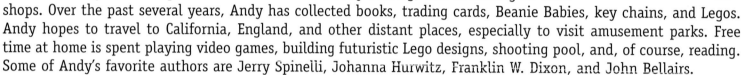

Rick Whipple received a B.F.A. in Graphic Design from Wichita State University in Wichita, Kansas, in 1975. He worked for several prestigious art studios before becoming a freelancer in 1983. In his twenty-five year career, Rick has worked in every area of illustration—advertising, editorial, book, and institutional. He specializes in depictions of people, but will take on almost any subject. He lives with his wife, Sara, and daughter, Audrey, in Old East Dallas, where he works from a garage-converted studio behind his house.